Black's Sketchbooks

London Adam & Charles Black

PUBLISHED BY

A. & C. BLACK · SOHO SQUARE · LONDON W.

LONDON

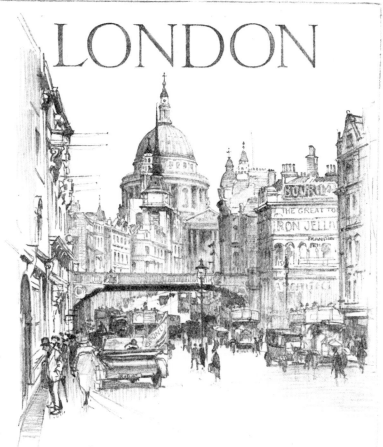

A SKETCH BOOK
BY DOROTHY E·G·WOOLLARD

A&C BLACK Ltd LONDON

LIST OF SKETCHES
BY
DOROTHY E·G·WOOLLARD.

WESTMINSTER ABBEY.

THE HOUSES OF PARLIAMENT.

THE CENOTAPH.

THE HORSE GUARDS

TRAFALGAR SQUARE

ST. MARTIN'S IN THE FIELDS.

PICCADILLY CIRCUS

PALL MALL.

HYDE PARK CORNER.

BUCKINGHAM PALACE.

WESTMINSTER CATHEDRAL ..

BROMPTON ORATORY.

THE BRITISH MUSEUM.

THE ROYAL EXCHANGE

WATERLOO BRIDGE.

BLACKFRIARS BRIDGE .   Dorothy Woollard .

SAINT PAULS

FISHMONGERS' HALL

TRAFFIC ON THE TOWER BRIDGE

Drawing of Woolwich .   THE TOWER BRIDGE .

Donald Maxwell

THE TOWER.

CLEOPATRAS NEEDLE.

First published in Great Britain in 1924
by A&C Black Publishers
36 Soho Square
London W1D 3QY
www.acblack.com

This edition published 2009

© 1924, 2009 A&C Black

ISBN 978-14081-1126-0

A CIP record of this book is available from the British Library

Printed and bound in China